BOSTON

IN PHOTOGRAPHS

BOSTON

IN PHOTOGRAPHS

In collaboration with the travel experts at Fodor's

Saba Alhadi

GRAMERCY BOOKS
NEW YORK

An imprint of **Chrysalis** Books Group plc

Published by Gramercy Books, an imprint of Random House
Value Publishing, a division of Random House, Inc.,
New York, by arrangement with Chrysalis Books, London.

Gramercy is a registered trademark and the colophon is a
trademark of Random House, Inc.

Random House
New York • Toronto • London • Sydney • Auckland
www.randomhouse.com

Printed and bound in China

A catalog record for this title is available from the Library of
Congress.

ISBN 0-517-22657-X

10 9 8 7 6 5 4 3 2 1

Credits

Editor: Anne McDowall
Designer: John Heritage
Picture Researcher: Rebecca Sodergren
Production: Kate Rogers
Reproduction: Anorax

Additional captions

Page 1: George Washington Statue, Boston Public Gardens
Page 2: Faneuil Hall Marketplace

Picture Acknowledgements

L=Left R=Right C=Center T=Top B= Bottom

© **Chrysalis Image Library** 48T, 68B, 71.
© **Corbis**: © Richard Cummins/CORBIS 18, 48B, 58B. / © Kevin
Fleming/CORBIS: 20B, 47, 55, 63. 74-75, 84, 89, 114T, 114B, 125. /
© Rick Friedman/Corbis 21, 93, 94, 117. / © Joel W.
Rogers/CORBIS 33. / © Richard T. Nowitz/CORBIS 39. / © Dave
G. Houser/CORBIS 87, 115. / © Ted Spiegel/CORBIS 92B. / © Lee
Snider/Photo Images/CORBIS 107, 119. / © Angelo
Hornak/CORBIS 109B. / © Farrell Grehan/CORBIS 112-113. / ©
Joseph Sohm; ChromoSohm Inc./CORBIS 116.
**Courtesy of the Gibson House Museum, Boston,
Massachusetts**. 26.

© **Lonely Planet Images** / Neil Setchfield 34, 105. / © Lonely
Planet Images / Kim Grant 36, 59, 72T, 76, 81, 90, 109T. / © Lonely
Planet Images/Angus Oborn. 124T.
© **Nichols House Museum** 46.
© **Photolibrary.com**: 1, 3, 68, 9, 10, 11, 12, 13, 14-15, 17, 19, 20T,
22, 24-25, 28-29, 30, 31, 40-41, 42, 43B, 49, 50-51 , 52, 53B, 53T,
56T, 57, 60, 62, 65, 66, 69, 77T, 79, 80, 97, 98, 99, 100-101, 102-103,
106, 108, 111   , 120, 121B, 122-123.
© **Saba K. Alhadi** 23, 27, 32, 35, 37T, 37B, 43T, 44T, 44B, 45, 48B,
56B, 58T, 61T, 61 ,64, 67T, 67B, 68T   72B, 73, 77B, 82T, 82B, 83,
85, 88T, 88B, 91T, 91B, 92T, 95, 121T, 124B.
© **Travelsite** / Neil Setchfield 110.

Contents

INTRODUCTION

The moment visitors arrive in Boston, they can see the old reflected in the new. Colonial landmarks stand in the shadow of modern skyscrapers, and narrow streets wind their way around busy highways. This is a compact city, steeped in history, art, and architecture. Boston was the birthplace of the American Revolution, and a walk along the Freedom Trail brings you to 16 famous sites integral to early American history. But the city has come a long way from its beginnings as a Puritan settlement, founded in 1630, and is now a cosmopolitan metropolis.

Boston's history is a story of how immigrants shaped a city. Long before the English arrived, the Massachusett Indian tribe lived on Boston's original

shoreline, the Shawmut Peninsula. In 1614, Captain John Smith mapped out an area and called it New England, and named the largest river Charles, after the British king. The Puritans arrived aboard the Mayflower, landing in Plymouth in 1620, and founded the first European settlement in New England.

In 1625, scholar and clergyman William Blackstone settled at the base of one of the three hills of the Shawmut Peninsula, Beacon Hill. He lived a solitary life for five years until he encouraged John Winthrop and a group of Puritans to relocate from Charlestown to Beacon Hill, promising them fresh water. John Winthrop soon became Boston's first governor, the town of Boston was founded, and the

bustling community forced William Blackstone to pack his belongings and leave Beacon Hill. John Winthrop named the Shawmut Peninsula Trimountaine, after the three hills, which were leveled years later and used for landfill. New settlers renamed the town Boston, after the small fishing village of the same name in Lincolnshire, England. Over the years, Boston has inspired a few nicknames that have remained to this day, notably Beantown and The Hub.

The British government had taken firm control of Boston by 1680. Looking to capitalize on its commerce, the Crown enforced tax laws to gain revenue. The Stamp Act of 1765 was the first direct tax on the colonies for mail and published materials. Rebellious colonists, led by John Hancock and Samuel Adams, protested against the taxes and the British occupation, and unrest provoked a series of uprisings among the American colonists. Tension escalated on March 5, 1770, when British soldiers opened fire on an angry mob right outside the Old State House. Although only five civilians died, the skirmish became known as the Boston Massacre.

On the evening of December 16, 1773, 5,000 angry Bostonians gathered at the Old South Meeting House to protest the controversial tea tax. When compromise failed, Samuel Adams signaled a group of patriots disguised as Indians to board the three ships carrying the tea, and dump 342 chests of tea into Boston Harbor. This event, which became known as the Boston Tea Party, was one of the turning points that led to the American Revolution. Today, Old South Meeting House is a museum that shows the multimedia presentation, *Voices of Protest*, which traces the turbulent history of the building as a gathering place for social reform over three centuries.

During the colonial era, rebel and silversmith Paul Revere closely monitored the movements of the British soldiers. He discovered that the Redcoats planned to march to Lexington, arrest John Hancock and Samuel Adams, and then seize ammunition stored in Concord. So, on April 18, 1775, Revere

◀ **Boston Skyline:** *Spectacular views of the Boston skyline can be seen from across the Charles River in Cambridge. Paul Revere and the British soldiers sailed across this river prior to the start of the American Revolution. Today, the Charles River is popular for recreational sailing, canoeing, and college rowing.*

▲ **Boston Skyline at Night:** *Boston's downtown offices light the night sky. The Custom House, with its illuminated clock, appears in between its neighboring skyscrapers. The large archway at Rowes Wharf comprises the Boston Harbor Hotel, offices, luxury condominiums, and a water shuttle to the airport.*

asked church sexton Robert Newman to hang two lanterns from Old North Church's steeple as a signal to the local militia, known as Minutemen, that the British soldiers were going to make their approach first by sea (crossing the Charles River) then march on to Lexington and Concord. He and fellow patriot William Dawes rode on horseback through the streets warning citizens to prepare for an imminent battle with the Redcoats. The "shot heard 'round the world" was fired in Lexington in the early morning hours of April 19, 1775. The American War of Independence had begun.

The war raged with intense fighting in and around Boston and throughout the 13 original colonies. One of the bloodiest battles was actually fought on Breed's Hill in Charlestown on June 17, 1775, but is commonly known as the Battle of

▶ **Springtime in Boston:** *The blooming magnolia trees along Commonwealth Avenue in the Back Bay are a sure sign of spring's arrival. The tree-lined promenade is designed to resemble a Parisian boulevard, with elegant Victorian mansions and townhouses, gardens, and statues.*

Bunker Hill. The British soldiers won the long and heated battle when the Minutemen exhausted their ammunition supplies. More than 1,000 British soldiers lost their lives, compared to 440 rebel forces.

Under the leadership of George Washington, victory for the colonists came on March 17, 1776, when British troops finally withdrew from the city that they had occupied for so long. In Philadelphia, on July 4, 1776, John Hancock was the first to sign the Declaration of Independence—and did so with a large signature so that King George III could read it without his eyeglasses. The Declaration of Independence was read to jubilant Bostonians on July 18, 1776, from the balcony of the Old State House, the same place from where Boston's royal governors had made their proclamations to the colonists years earlier.

Boston's renaissance began in the early nineteenth century. Descendants of the Puritans became wealthy Boston Brahmins, lived in Beacon Hill, and were influential in political, social, and economic reform. Prominent architect Charles Bulfinch changed the appearance of the city with his trademark red-brick Federalist design on aristocratic homes and public buildings. Demand for more housing resulted in building on top of landfill in 1858 and 40 years later, new neighborhoods such as Back Bay and the South End emerged.

Boston was in the forefront of the anti-slavery movement, and by 1800 the city was home to the nation's largest free black community. The African Meeting House, now the Museum of Afro-American History, became the nation's first black church in 1809 on the northern slope of Beacon Hill. The area became part of the Underground Railroad network, and abolitionists used their Beacon Hill homes as safe havens for fugitive slaves.

Shiploads of European immigrants began to dock in Boston in the mid-nineteenth century. The Irish, who arrived in 1845 to escape the potato famine, overcame adversity to become a strong

▶ **Leonard P. Zakim Bunker Hill Bridge:** *Completed in 2002 as part of the Big Dig project, the Leonard P. Zakim Bunker Hill Bridge stretches over the Charles River with no support columns below. The sleek structure—the widest suspension bridge in the world—links Charlestown to other areas of Boston.*

▼ **Freedom Trail Plaque:** *Established in 1951, the Freedom Trail meanders 2.5 miles along Boston's sidewalks to connect 16 historic sites. Metal plaques like this one outside Faneuil Hall, along with inlaid brick and overlaid red paint, identify the Trail's route.*

political force in Boston for many years. Other immigrants—Italians, Germans, Russians, Polish, Portuguese, and Asians—also found jobs and financial security here. The majority of Boston's population in 1860 consisted of immigrants, who eventually carved out communities in the North End, Chinatown, Charlestown, and South Boston.

In the first half of the twentieth century, the economic infrastructure began a steady decline due to corrupt politics and an increasing crime rate. Boston lost its waterfront trade to San Francisco and Seattle, and the manufacturing sector moved to the southern states. But in 1957, the economic tide turned with urban renewal projects, the restructur-

ing of the city aided by billions of dollars of government funding. The economy prospered in the 1960s, and new buildings began to define Boston's skyline: the Prudential Tower in 1964, and the John Hancock Tower, Boston's tallest building, in 1976.

By the mid-1980s, Boston's rejuvenated economy was being touted as "The Massachusetts Miracle" by the media, and in the same decade, local planners devised the Big Dig, the complex engineering project intended to redesign the city's major highways and place them underground. Construction began in 1991 and is still ongoing. The Big Dig is the most expensive public works project in history, having cost the city $15 billion to date. Two of the Big Dig's major successes are the Ted Williams Tunnel and the Leonard P. Zakim Bunker Hill Bridge, which is the widest suspension bridge in the world,

Mass transportation originated in Boston in 1897. The public transportation system is known as the "T" and is the most convenient way to travel throughout Boston and Cambridge: subways, buses, ferries, and commuter trains move 1.2 million passengers a day. The subway system is divided into five lines stretching from downtown Boston and into the suburbs.

Every September more than 200,000 students descend upon Boston to attend one of more than 60 colleges and universities. Two of the most prestigious universities in the world, Harvard University and

Massachusetts Institute of Technology (MIT), are just across the Charles River in Cambridge. The student population gives Harvard Square, Kenmore Square, and the Fenway area an energetic, youthful presence.

Boston offers a wealth of attractions any time of the year. One of the best times to visit is in the fall, when the summer crowds have abated and the leaves have a colorful glow against the autumn sky. Spring brings the tulips out in the Public Garden and the magnolia-tree blossoms on Commonwealth Avenue in the Back Bay. It's no wonder that millions of people visit Boston to relive American history, capture the city's spirit, and walk away with a great cultural experience.

▼ **Acorn Street:** *This quaint, narrow cobblestone street with its nineteenth-century brick rowhouses is the most photographed street in Boston. Some of these homes were once occupied by artisans and shopkeepers, while others were used as horse stables.*

▶ **Charles River** *The Charles River separates Boston from Cambridge. The riverfront includes the Esplanade, playgrounds, and jogging trails. Sailing, canoeing, and college rowing are popular, too, and the Head of Charles Regatta is the world's largest rowing event.*

▶ **Harvard Business School:** *Harvard University is the oldest college in America, founded in 1636 with only nine students. Today, Harvard is world-renowned for its academic excellence and has more than 18,000 degree candidates, and 400 buildings scattered throughout Boston and Cambridge. Famous graduates include poet Henry David Thoreau and President John F. Kennedy.*

Back Bay & South End

Whether it's shopping, dining, art, architecture, or people watching, Boston's Back Bay district is where you'll find it. But this cosmopolitan metropolis has a historic secret: it was once swampland! Back Bay was built on landfill in 1856 and completed 40 years later. Architect Arthur Gilman designed the area to be reminiscent of Paris, with wide, elegant boulevards and Victorian buildings. A fashionable neighborhood emerged, with streets laid out in a grid-like pattern—a clear departure from the narrow, winding alleyways of Boston's colonial past. Ironically, streets were named after English dukes and earls in alphabetical order.

Copley Square is the heart of Back Bay. Named for famous eighteenth-century portrait painter John Singleton Copley, the plaza is anchored by Trinity Church and the Boston Public Library, both architectural marvels. Boston's tallest building, the John Hancock Tower, looms over Copley Square, providing interesting reflections in its shiny blue-mirrored windows. Music festivals and a weekly farmer's market take place in summer, and enormous ice sculptures are displayed every New Year's Eve.

A stroll along Newbury Street lures visitors to the Back Bay's upscale and trendy shops, hip art galleries, outdoor cafés, and ethnic restaurants. The ambiance is more sophisticated towards the Arlington Street end, while there's a more laid-back vibe near Massachusetts Avenue. Newbury Street is definitely a place to see and be seen.

Boylston Street separates Newbury Street and Copley Square. Architecture enthusiasts might find the Romanesque-style façade of Boylston Fire Station, the city's first police and fire station, of interest. Boylston Street is the finishing point for the legendary Boston Marathon every April and a granite map of the nation's oldest foot race is embedded in Boylston Street, near Dartmouth Street.

Back Bay's grand residential street is Commonwealth Avenue, an example of nineteenth-century Victorian architecture at its finest. It is most picturesque in the spring when the magnolias are in bloom, but year-round this tree-lined promenade is a popular stroll for locals, tourists, and dogs alike.

A five-minute walk south of Copley Square brings you to the South End. The neighborhood retains much of charm with its rows of Victorian homes with elaborate cast-iron railings in the Union Park area, and trendy bistros and outdoor cafés scattered about. The hip crowds dine at many of the eateries on Washington Street, while casual diners prefer Charlie's Sandwich Shoppe on Columbus Avenue, a 1930's time-capsule restaurant.

The center of the South End's booming art scene is the SoWa Building on Harrison Avenue. Start on the third floor and wander down to the small galleries of unusual works of art. The Boston Center for the Arts—a landmark building on Tremont Street, which in the nineteenth century was an organ factory —is now filled with galleries displaying a mix of eclectic and contemporary art.

The best way to explore Back Bay and the South End is on foot—it's bursting with cultural attractions waiting to be discovered.

▶ **John Hancock Tower:** *Designed by I.M. Pei in 1976, the John Hancock Tower is the tallest building in New England. Soon after the tower was constructed, 65 windows weighing 500 pounds each crashed to the ground. All 10,344 windows were replaced before the building opened. The office building stands 790 feet tall with 60 floors, and a mirrored façade that reflects its surroundings and sky.*

IN HONOR
OF THE
ACHUSETTS VOLUNTEER INFANTRY
IN REMEMBRANCE OF THE
S AND MEN WHO FELL IN ITS RANKS
NT HAS BEEN GIVEN TO THE CITY OF BOSTON

◀ **Courtyard of the Boston Public Library:** *The nation's first public library has an Italian-inspired cloistered courtyard in the center of the building. The courtyard provides a quiet place to read or relax away from the sounds of the city.*

▲ **Boston Public Library:** *Founded in 1848, the Boston Public Library was the first library in America. The Italian Renaissance-style building, which overlooks Copley Square, carries 6.1 million books. The library's collection includes rare folios by William Shakespeare and original music scores by Mozart. The exquisite interior features murals by famous artists that wind up the grand marble staircase.*

◄ **Prudential Center:** *The Prudential Tower reigned as Boston's tallest building from 1964 until the John Hancock Tower was built in 1976. The modern Prudential Center complex offers more than 75 shops and a variety of dining options. In the foreground is the Belvedere Condominium.*

◄ **View from Skywalk Observatory:** *The Skywalk Observatory on the 50th floor of the Prudential Tower offers breathtaking panoramic views of Boston and Cambridge from 700 feet in the air. Huge windows are marked to help locate city attractions.*

► **Copley Square:** *Beautiful architecture surrounds the picturesque Copley Square plaza at the heart of Back Bay. Seen here is Trinity Church; other buildings facing the square include Boston Public Library and the John Hancock Tower.*

◀ **Christian Science**
Center: *The world head-*
quarters of the Christian
Science Church is located on
the corner of Huntington and
Massachusetts Avenues. The
28-story, granite,
Romanesque-style Mother
Church was built in 1894 and
is home to its administrative
offices and the Christian
Science Monitor, *the church's*
popular newspaper. The
complex occupies 14 acres
and features a huge plaza
with a 700-foot reflecting pool.

▲ **Boylston Fire**
Station: *Built in 1887 and*
designed in the Romanesque
style, the Boylston Fire Station
(right) was the city's first
combined fire and police
station and housed the first
ladder truck in Boston. In
1976, the police station was
renovated into galleries and
became the Institute of
Contemporary Art (left).

**Trinity Church:**
*Consistently voted one
of America's ten finest
architectural buildings, Trinity
Church was designed by
Henry Hobson Richardson
and completed in 1877.
The Romanesque structure
was built on 4,500 wooden
pilings driven through Back
Bay's landfill to support the
granite foundation. Trinity
is an Episcopal church
with approximately 3,700
parishioners.*

◀ **Gibson House**

Museum: *The Gibson House was one of the first homes built on Beacon Street in Boston's Back Bay in 1859. The brownstone's redbrick façade was designed in the Italian Renaissance Revival style. Each of its six stories preserves original Victorian décor and furnishings of the 1860s, making it an authentic time-capsule.*

▲ **Newbury Street:**

Boston's elegant shopping district, Newbury Street, is lined with chic boutiques, outdoor cafés, and exclusive art galleries. There are nearly 40 galleries on Newbury Street, specializing in art from antiques to contemporary.

▶▶ **Commonwealth**

Avenue: *Back Bay's Victorian residential neighborhood, Commonwealth Avenue, is a 100-foot wide boulevard framed by elm trees and lined with statues from Boston's history. Once a promenade for aristocrats, the mall is still a great place for a leisurely stroll.*

◀ **Boston Public Garden:** *Founded in 1837, the Public Garden was the first botanical garden in America. A group of Bostonians transformed marshland into a garden filled with tulips, roses, and Boston's first poinsettia plant. Today, its 24 acres display colorful flowerbeds, weeping-willow trees, and a three-acre lagoon. Popular attractions include the Swan Boats and the "Make Way for Ducklings" sculpture.*

▲ **George Washington Statue:** *The first equestrian statue of George Washington watches passersby enter Boston's beautiful Public Garden from Arlington Street. The statue, by Thomas Ball, was dedicated in 1869.*

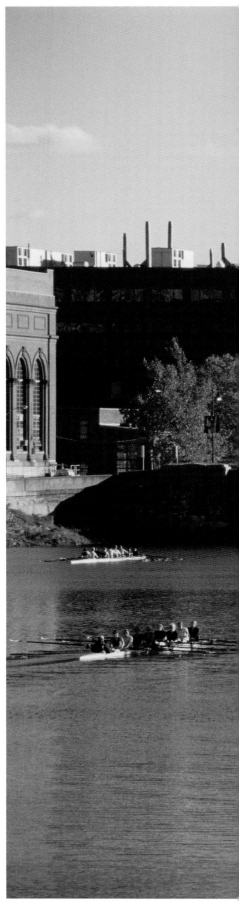

▲ **Swan Boats:** *The world-famous Swan Boats of Boston have graced the Public Garden's lagoon since 1877. Designed by English immigrant Robert Paget, the six pedal-propelled boats gently circle the small pond while ducks swim alongside. The Swan Boats were immortalized in the 1941 children's classic,* Make Way for Ducklings

▶ **The Esplanade:** *On the east side of the Charles River are a series of lagoons, islands, and parkland running perpendicular to Back Bay's streets. Known as The Esplanade, the area is a great place for strolling, jogging, cycling, and rollerblading. The Hatch Shell on The Esplanade is used for music concerts and the annual Fourth of July performance by the Boston Pops.*

◀ **First Baptist Church:** *Built in the Romanesque style and designed by architect Henry Hobson Richardson, the First Baptist Church became an instant landmark in Back Bay in 1872. The square tower has a decorative frieze with trumpeting angels on the corners and carved likenesses of Henry Wadsworth Longfellow, Ralph Waldo Emerson, and other prominent Bostonians.*

▲ **Union Park:** *Once home to European immigrants, this trendy neighborhood has a broadly mixed population. Bow-fronted, red-brick brownstones with bay windows are typical of South End's Union Park. The prized nineteenth-century ornamental ironwork is especially intriguing.*

◀ **Boston Center for the Arts:** *A complex that includes galleries, three theaters, the Boston Ballet Building, artists' studios, and rehearsal space. The largest of the center's buildings is the Cyclorama, opened in 1884 to exhibit the huge painting* The Battle of Gettysburg *by Frenchman Paul Philippoteaux.*

▶ **New Old South Church:** *Parishioners who previously worshipped at Old South Meeting House on downtown's Washington Street built this church on Copley Square in 1874–5. The Italian Gothic-style architecture, tall bell tower, and brown, pink, and gray stonework are distinguishing features.*

▶ **SoWa Building:** *Once a warehouse, the SoWa building in the South End has emerged as the center of Boston's art-gallery scene. Most galleries are run independently by artists and feature unusual work with a focus on contemporary art, sculpture, photography, and multimedia art.*

Beacon Hill

The grandeur of Old Boston can be found in Beacon Hill, one of the city's most exclusive neighborhoods. Picturesque streets, brick sidewalks, old-fashioned gas lamps, antique purple windows, decorative iron balconies, and unique doors and door-knockers adorning nineteenth-century brownstones make Beacon Hill a fascinating area to explore.

In the late eighteenth century, the Mount Vernon Proprietors commissioned Charles Bulfinch, Boston's foremost architect, to design homes on undeveloped land they purchased from portrait artist John Singleton Copley. The dramatic change in Beacon Hill's architecture attracted aristocratic families, poets, and authors. Louisburg Square became the most coveted address in Boston and the square's elegant red-brick brownstones arranged around a gated private park still contain Boston's highest priced properties.

Boston's elite also occupied Federalist-style mansions, like the Prescott House on Beacon Street. The Nichols House Museum on Mount Vernon Street is furnished with oriental rugs and nineteenth-century art. Pinckney Street has the oldest house on Beacon Hill, the George Middleton House, as well as the House of Odd Windows and some hidden homes and gardens. Acorn Street, with its quaint brick rowhouses on a tiny cobblestone lane, is the most photographed street in Boston.

Interestingly, the black community also lived in Beacon Hill, near their employers on the North Slope of the Hill. Several white residents played an important role in the anti-slavery movement and harbored fugitive slaves. The African Meeting House and the Museum of Afro-American History on Joy Street display exhibits from that era.

The magnificent Massachusetts State House on Beacon Street stands prominently on land that was once John Hancock's cow pasture! Designed by Charles Bulfinch and modeled after Somerset House in London, the State House was completed in 1798. Its shiny gold dome is one of Boston's most well-known landmarks. Originally sheathed in copper by Paul Revere and Sons, the dome now has a 23-carat gold covering. Free tours of the State House are given on weekdays. Nearby is the Boston Athenaeum, a beautiful private library containing some of George Washington's books. Opposite the State House is the Shaw Memorial, a bronze sculpture that depicts Robert Gould Shaw proudly leading the first all-black regiment to battle during the Civil War in 1863. The Shaw Memorial is a popular starting point for the Freedom Trail.

▶ **Acorn Street:** *As the most photographed street in Boston, Acorn Street attracts many visitors with its charming brick rowhouses on a narrow cobblestone street. Built in 1828, the homes were once used as horse stables, while others were residences of shopkeepers and servants.*

◀ **Beacon Hill:** *Beacon Hill is an impressive nineteenth-century neighborhood rich in history and architecture. Grand homes, charming streets, brick sidewalks, gas lamps, hidden houses, unique doors and doorknockers make Beacon Hill a great place for a walk in a bygone era.*

▲ **Beacon Street:** *The steepest part of Beacon Street, near the Massachusetts State House, was laid out in 1640. Nineteenth-century Victorian homes line this bustling street. Early Bostonians believed that the summit of the hills provided a healthy atmosphere; therefore, the higher the ascent, the older the house.*

▶ **House of Odd Windows, Pinckney Street:** *Ralph Waldo Emerson's nephew designed this 1884 house with uniqueness so that every window is different, yet proportionately placed. A rooftop eyelid window peeks over at passersby.*

▼ **Louisburg Square:** *Built in the mid-nineteenth century, exclusive Louisburg Square is reminiscent of classic London residences, with red-brick, bow-fronted façades in the Greek Revival architectural style. The Christmas traditions of candle-lit windows, strolling carolers, and hand-bell ringers originated in Louisburg Square.*

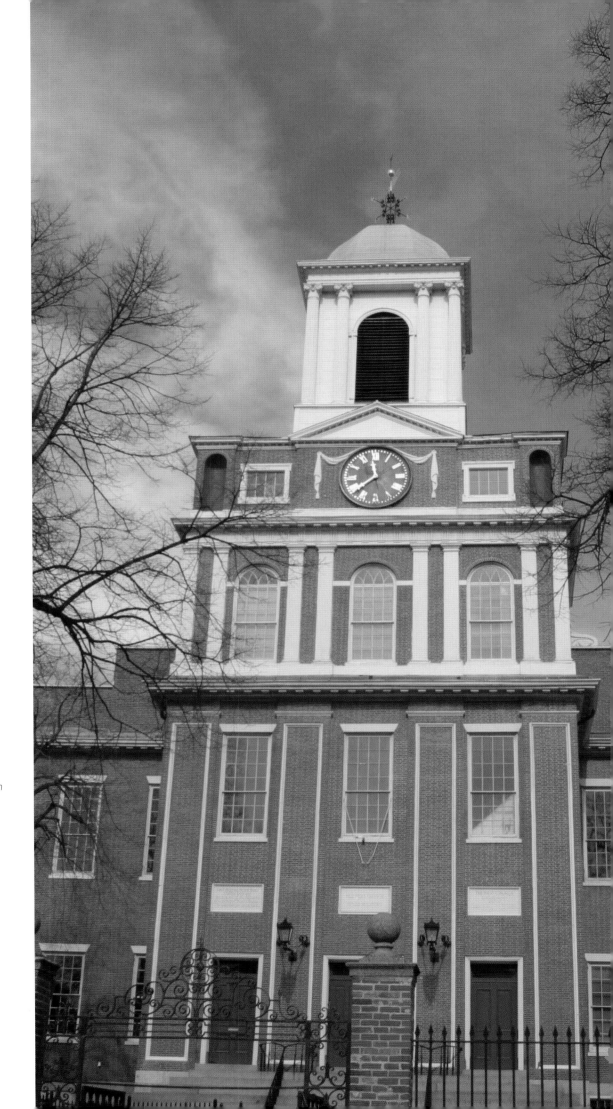

◀ **Chestnut Street:**
The residences on Chestnut Street were designed in the Charles Bulfinch Federal architectural style, with arched doorways and gabled roofs. The famed antique purple windows adorn a few homes. The Harvard Musical Association, on the corner of Chestnut and West Cedar Streets, is the nation's oldest music library.

▶ **Old West Church:**
The British used Old West Church as a barracks for soldiers prior to the Revolutionary War. Its red-brick façade and ornamental clocks on the sides of the tower are landmarks, while inside is a pipe organ often played in classical organ recordings.

◀ **George Middleton House:** *Built in 1797, this house is the oldest wooden structure on Beacon Hill. George Middleton, a black Revolutionary war soldier, and his friend Louis Glapion lived here for a year before Glapion got married. The house was then divided in two vertically so that each occupant had half the house.*

◀ **Nichols House
Museum:** *This Bulfinch-
designed house was occupied
by eccentric spinster Rose
Nichols from 1885 to 1960,
and furnished with lavish
oriental rugs and priceless art.
The museum offers a glimpse
into the life of Boston's elite in
the late nineteenth century.*

▲ **Harrison Gray Otis House Museum:** *Charles Bulfinch designed this 1796 Federal-style mansion for his friend, statesman Harrison Gray Otis. Furnished in early nineteenth-century style, the museum offers an interesting picture of the lifestyle of wealthy Bostonians.*

◀ **African Meeting House:** *An impressive building with tall, arched windows, the African Meeting House was built by African-Americans in 1806 and is the oldest surviving black church in America. It played an important role in the anti-slavery movement in the nineteenth century.*

▼ **Museum of Afro-American History:** *The African Meeting House and the adjacent Abiel Smith School—the first black grammar school, founded in 1835— together form the most valuable assets at the Museum of Afro-American History.*

▶ **Boston Athenaeum:**
Founded in 1807 by 14
Boston gentlemen, this
beautiful private library
contains some of George
Washington's books and
other works of art. It helped
establish Boston's Museum
of Fine Arts and houses
an extensive collection of
books on New England
history, English and American
literature, and decorative arts.

▶▶ **Massachusetts**
State House: *The oldest*
building on Beacon Hill was
built in 1795 and designed by
prominent architect Charles
Bulfinch. The gold dome has a
23-carat gold-leaf covering.
The State House became the
seat of government shortly
after the American Revolution.

◄ **Shaw Memorial:**

This bronze sculpture portrays Robert Gould Shaw leading the first all-black volunteer regiment to battle during the Civil War. Shaw and 62 members of his troop were killed on July 19, 1863, in an assault on Fort Wagner, South Carolina.

▶ **Cheers Restaurant:**

Officially known as the Bull and Finch Bar, the bar was the setting for the popular sitcom Cheers. Producers decided that the exterior defined it as a neighborhood pub and the still-hanging Cheers sign opened every episode of the show.

▶ **Museum of Science and Science Park:**

Highlights at the Museum of Science, which has interactive exhibits oriented to families, include Tyrannosaurus rex, stairs that sing when you step on them, and the Big Dig Exhibit. The planetarium hosts celestial laser shows, while the Omni Theater shows IMAX® films on nature and history on a five-story wraparound screen.

Colonial Boston

In the shadow of skyscrapers, Boston's colonial past has been preserved in the actual sites where historic events took place. The city was first settled by the Puritans, the predecessors of the rebellious patriots, who struggled for independence from British occupation. Boston's history is best explored on the Freedom Trail, a two-and-a-half-mile stretch marked by inlaid bricks and red paint linking significant landmarks that played an important role in the American Revolution.

Nearly half of the Freedom Trail's 16 sites are in downtown Boston. Boston Common, America's first public park, is a good starting point. Purchased in 1634 from Boston's first occupant, William Blaxton, it became a cow pasture and military training ground. Once the site of colonial protests, public hangings, and burials, the Common is now used for public events, concerts, picnics, and strolls.

Overlooking Boston Common is Park Street Church, the first landmark immigrants saw upon arriving in Boston in the early nineteenth century. Adjacent to the church is the Old Granary Burying Ground. This 1660 cemetery is the resting place for the five victims of the Boston Massacre, and patriots Samuel Adams, John Hancock, and Paul Revere.

King's Chapel was founded in 1686 as the first Anglican church in America. In 1749, the wooden building was dismantled and redesigned as the current stone church. Visitors can tour its elegant interior. The adjoining King's Chapel Burying Ground is the oldest cemetery in Boston, founded in 1630.

Old City Hall on School Street was built in 1862 on the former site of Boston Latin School, America's first public school, established in 1635. The 1856 statue of Benjamin Franklin in front of the building was the first portrait statue erected in the U.S. At the end of School Street is the Old Corner Bookstore, a 1718 brick building, which was once Boston's first pharmacy and later a thriving literary center. Opposite is the Old South Meeting House, a church where thousands of colonists gathered on December 16, 1773, before participating in what came to be known as the Boston Tea Party.

The Old State House is overshadowed by tall office buildings, yet stands prominently on the corner of Washington and State Streets. Built in 1713, this brick building was the site of many confrontations that lead to the American Revolution. The Boston Massacre took place right outside it in 1773, near the balcony from which the Declaration of Independence was proudly read on July 18, 1776.

Wealthy merchant Peter Faneuil bestowed a gift of a common marketplace to Boston in 1742. Faneuil Hall was nicknamed the "Cradle of Liberty" because it became the gathering place to hear patriot speakers John Hancock and Samuel Adams rebel against the Crown. In 1805, Charles Bulfinch enlarged Faneuil Hall to its present size after a fire destroyed the interior in 1761. Just behind Faneuil Hall is Quincy Market, once Boston's major fish and meat market. It is now a three-building structure that houses numerous eateries, shops, and pushcarts selling a variety of specialty items. The most popular tourist destination in Boston, Faneuil Hall and Quincy Market, also known as Faneuil Hall Marketplace, is filled with tourists, musicians, mimes, and jugglers in the summer.

▶ **Interior of Quincy Market:** *Built in 1822, the granite Quincy Market building stands in stark contrast with Faneuil Hall's brick exterior. It is two stories high and more than 500 feet long. The central part of the building's interior has a large copper dome and rotunda rising high above the dining crowds below.*

BOLTON & HICKS

H. A. HOVEY CO.
BUTTER-EGGS-CHEESE

HOLLAND

JULIUS LANSKY & SON

COLLEY FOODS CO.

37 ADAMS CHAPMAN C

STOR

KET OF THE CITY SINCE ITS DEDICATION IN AUGUS

LEAN
CO., INC.
-PORK-LAMB

comedy

◄ **Old Granary Burying Ground:** *Established in 1660, the third-oldest cemetery in Boston is the final resting place for the five victims of the Boston Massacre as well as patriots Samuel Adams, John Hancock, and Paul Revere. The cemetery's name is derived from the grain warehouse once at the site of adjacent Park Street Church.*

◄ **Boston Common:**
Originally a cow pasture, the oldest public park in America was founded in 1634. The Common has been the site of colonial protests, public hangings, and burials, and British troops camped out and trained here. Today it is a gathering place for public events, concerts, picnics, and strolls.

► **Park Street Church:**
Built in 1809, Park Street Church was once the first landmark immigrants saw upon arriving in Boston. The church was the site of anti-slavery speeches in the nineteenth century and was once known as Brimstone Corner because of gunpowder stored there for the War of 1812.

King's Chapel: *The first Anglican church in America was built on the town's only cemetery in 1686. Rebuilt as a stone church in 1749, it was the place of worship for British soldiers. Its interior has original high box pews and the oldest pulpit in the country. Money ran out before construction of the church was completed, so a spire was never added.*

Omni Parker House: *One of the oldest hotels in America, the Omni Parker House, which opened in 1855, attracted wealthy patrons and was a gathering place for famous American writers. Baseball legends Ted Williams and Babe Ruth often dined here. Boston Cream Pie was first created in the hotel's kitchen in 1871.*

King's Chapel Burying Ground: *As the oldest cemetery in Boston, King's Chapel Burying Ground contains the graves of nearly all of Boston's early settlers, the Puritans, who were buried next to an Anglican church. Boston's first governor, John Winthrop, is buried here, as is Mary Chilton, the first woman to step off the Mayflower in 1620.*

◀ **Old South Meeting House:** *This 1729 building was the largest building in town to accommodate angry colonists when crowds overflowed at Faneuil Hall. In 1773, Samuel Adams led the meeting that protested the tea tax, which prompted the Boston Tea Party. The building, which has served as church, a post office, and a British stable, is now a museum with interactive exhibits.*

▶ **Old Corner Bookstore:** *Boston's first pharmacy was on the street level of this 1718 brick building. Publishers Ticknor & Fields transformed it into a successful literary center. Nathaniel Hawthorne's* The Scarlet Letter *and Henry David Thoreau's* Walden *were published here. The building is owned by Historic Boston Inc., a group who saved it from demolition in 1960.*

▶ **Old City Hall:** *The elegant 1865 building designed in the French Second Empire style was built on the former site of the first public school in America, Boston Latin. Old City Hall was used as one of the first examples of how to successfully renovate old public buildings. It served as Boston's City Hall until 1969 and now houses offices.*

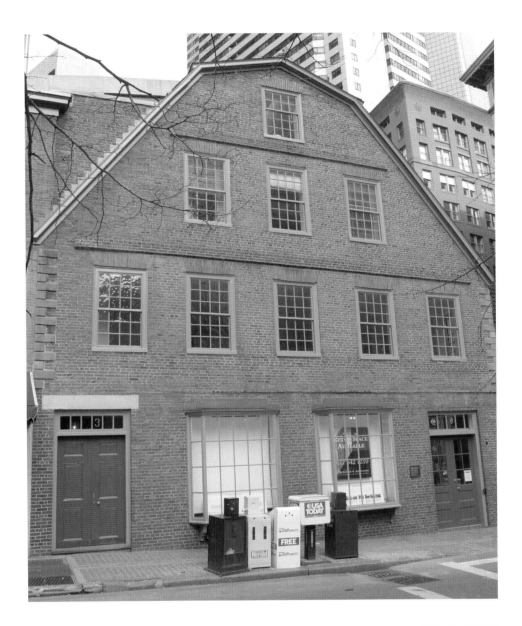

Old State House: *In the shadow of tall buildings stands the former the headquarters of the British government. Built in 1713, Old State House later became the first seat of government in Massachusetts.*

Today, it is a museum that houses exhibits on early Boston history to the present. Every year on the Fourth of July, the Declaration of Independence is read from the balcony here, as it has been since 1776.

Site of the Boston Massacre: *A ring of cobblestones embedded in a small traffic island in front of the Old State House balcony marks the site of the Boston Massacre, where five colonists died in a skirmish with British*

soldiers on March 5, 1770. Patriot lawyers John Adams and Josiah Quincy defended the eight British soldiers involved in the riot.

◄ **Irish Famine Memorial:** *This memorial, erected in 1998, commemorates the 150th anniversary of the Irish Famine, and portrays Irish immigrants in Boston and their triumph over adversity. Boston is considered the first Irish capital of America, and there are nearly 44 million Irish-Americans living in the U.S. today.*

▶ **Faneuil Hall Marketplace:** *Faneuil Hall once echoed with the sounds of angry protesters during the colonial era. Quincy Market is just behind it, and together, they comprise Faneuil Hall Marketplace, an area full of energy, crowds, shops, food and street performers, and undoubtedly the most popular destination in Boston.*

Holocaust Memorial: *The six 50-foot-high, hollow glass towers etched with six million numbers pay tribute to the victims of the Holocaust. Built to resemble smokestacks, the columns symbolize the six major Nazi concentration camps and have engraved quotations from survivors of the tragedy. Steam rising from the grates beneath the pillars makes a haunting scene at night.*

Bell in Hand Tavern: *A former town crier originally opened the oldest tavern in America in 1795 on Congress Street. This busy bar is now next to the Union Oyster House and attracts locals and tourists alike with live music and its own signature beer. Windows open out to the street for an al-fresco feel in the summer.*

Faneuil Hall: *Wealthy merchant Peter Faneuil bestowed a gift of a common marketplace to Boston in 1742. Political meetings were held on the second floor, where rebellious patriots boycotted English imports and the occupation. The building is topped by its landmark weathervane, a copper grasshopper. The restored meeting hall now has souvenir shops and exhibits on colonial history.*

◀ **Durgin Park:** *Durgin Park's menu of traditional New England food hasn't changed much since the restaurant opened in 1827. Boston Baked Beans, Yankee pot roast, corned beef and cabbage, and Indian pudding are served in large portions by surly staff—part of the restaurant's gimmick. The communal tables complement the casual atmosphere.*

▶ **Custom House:** *The 26-story Custom House was built in 1847 to collect customs revenue. For 30 years, the building was Boston's first skyscraper. Its distinctive clock is a city landmark and falcons still make their nest inside the clock tower. The observation deck on the top floor offers spectacular panoramic views of Boston and its environs.*

◀ **Union Oyster House:** *Located just outside Faneuil Hall Marketplace, the oldest continuously operating restaurant in Boston opened in 1826. New England seafood such as Boston scrod, lobster, and clam chowder are served in a lively atmosphere with Old World décor. John F. Kennedy was a frequent diner, and his favorite booth is dedicated to his memory.*

Chinatown & Theater District

Behind the Financial District's skyscrapers is the nation's first Chinatown. Like many areas of Boston, it was built on landfill. The first wave of Chinese immigrants came by ship to New England from San Francisco in 1870. An economic boom in the 1880s prompted another wave of Chinese immigrants seeking job opportunities in construction, on the railroad, and laying telephone lines, and by the early twentieth century, Chinatown had become a firmly established enclave of Boston. Currently, there is a diverse Asian population of approximately 8,000 and more than 200 businesses here.

The elaborate Chinatown Gate welcomes visitors to experience Asian culture. There's an abundance of Chinese restaurants, bakeries, and tea-houses, as well as Japanese, Korean, and Vietnamese eateries. Specialty shops sell everything from traditional Chinese medicine to jade jewelry, while the food markets sell a variety of fresh seafood, Asian vegetables, and live poultry. Adding character to the area are pagoda-topped telephone booths and Chinese characters on most storefronts. Chinatown is known for its festive and colorful parades: the annual Harvest Moon Festival and the Boston Chinatown Festival are celebrated in August, the Asian Food Festival takes place in October, and the Chinese New Year Banquet kicks off in January.

Close to Chinatown is the Theater District, where Boston's first theater opened in 1793. Once the site of more than 30 theaters, Boston became a major pre-Broadway tryout spot. Many American musicals premiered in here, including *A Streetcar Named Desire* and *Oklahoma!* Though most of the opulent theaters have gone, three major venues—the Wang Center for the Performing Arts, Colonial Theater, and Shubert Theater—still feature touring productions and Broadway hits. The Boston Opera House was built in 1928 on the site of the original Boston Theate, which was internationally recognized until financial difficulties forced it to close in 1991. The landmark Opera House reopened after a multi-million dollar restoration in the summer of 2004. Disney's *Lion King* was its inaugural production.

Downtown Crossing is a bustling commercial district located on the original landmass of colonial Boston, and some street patterns date back to the seventeenth century. Today's Washington Street was once the main road in old Boston and is now lined with a number of retail outlets. Contrasting architectural styles are seen in the two major department stores, the Modernist style of Macy's and the Beaux-Arts Filene's. Beneath the latter is the chaotic Filene's Basement, which is well known for quality merchandise at bargain prices.

▶ **Boston Opera House:** *The landmark Boston Opera House built in 1928 beautifies Downtown Crossing with its grand Spanish Baroque façade and majestic interior. Reopened in 2004 after a multi-million-dollar renovation, the Opera House welcomed Disney's* Lion King *as its inaugural production.*

Brattle Book Shop:
The country's oldest continuously operating used bookstore—it opened in 1825—is packed with more than 250,000 rare books, old magazines, postcards, greeting cards, and antique maps. The three-story building is a great place in which to browse for bargain books as well..

◀ **Downtown Crossing:**

Downtown Crossing is a busy shopping district with Filene's and Macy's as the two major department stores. The district has gone through many architectural changes, and some of its retail outlets are now housed in restored old buildings.

▲ **Shubert Theater:**

The handsome, white, Neo-classical façade of the Shubert Theater flanks a Palladian-style window over the entrance. The theater, which opened its doors in 1910, is listed on the National Register for Historic Places.

◄ **Colonial Theater:**
Boston's oldest theater opened on December 20, 1920 with Ben Hur. *Today the theater is renowned for musical productions. The theater's impressive interior features elegant chandeliers and high, arched ceilings.*

◀ **Jacob Wirth's:**
Boston's second oldest restaurant is in the heart of the theater district. The popular Jacob Wirth's hasn't changed much since it opened for business in 1868. Traditional German food is served on mahogany tables in an old-fashioned beer hall.

▶ **Chinatown street scene:** The Asian influence is prominent in Boston's colourful Chinatown, where Chinese characters still identify restaurants, food markets, bakeries, and teahouses. Though the area is not very large, it was the first Chinatown to be established in the United States.

▶ **Wang Center for the Performing Arts:**
New England's most lavish theater opened in 1925, inspired by the Paris Opera House. With more than 3,600 seats, the Wang Center hosts an array of Broadway shows, dance, opera, and film. This view shows the lobby ceiling.

The Waterfront

In the 1620s, English immigrants sailed to the New World via Boston Harbor, the oldest continuously active seaport in the country. The Waterfront quickly prospered through shipping and trade, and continued to do so for hundreds of years. In 1773, Boston Harbor was the scene of the Boston Tea Party, one of the turning points that led to the American Revolution, when colonists disguised as Mohawk Indians dumped 342 chests of tea into the water to protest the high tax on tea during British occupation.

Several wharves fringe Boston Harbor's 43-mile coastline. Long Wharf, the oldest continuously operated wharf in America, was built in 1710 to accommodate maritime commerce. Now located behind Faneuil Hall Marketplace, Long Wharf once extended 2,000 feet into Boston Harbor from near the Old State House on State Street. Rowes Wharf replaced a pair of wharves built in the 1760s. It is now a modern development comprised of the luxurious Boston Harbor Hotel, pricey condominiums, offices, and a marina operating a water shuttle to Logan International Airport.

For many years Bostonians avoided the Waterfront because it was a noisy, industrial wasteland. Despite the polluted waters, the city began renovating old wharf buildings into apartments in the 1960s. The turning point in the Waterfront's history came in 1986, when a massive cleanup transformed the area into a tourist attraction. Visitors come to the Waterfront for leisurely strolls, ferries to the Boston Harbor islands, or to dine at one of the many great seafood restaurants here. Private yachts and sailboats enhance the waterfront's elegant backdrop.

The New England Aquarium is a prime attraction on Central Wharf. Designed to introduce visitors to aquatic life, the aquarium was built around the four-story, 200,000-gallon Giant Ocean Tank, which is filled with sharks, huge sea turtles, sting rays, and exotic fish. Almost all of the balconies overlook the indoor Penguin Exhibit, home to colonies of adorable penguins from all over the world.

The Boston Children's Museum is a fun place where children enjoy numerous interactive exhibits such as a rock-climbing wall, grocery shopping in an ethnic market, or exploring Japanese family life in a two-story home. Nearby is one of Boston's most unusual museums, the Boston Fire Museum. Once an old firehouse, the museum exhibits antique fire-fighting equipment, photo displays, and fire-alarm artifacts.

Christopher Columbus Park is the best place to relax and enjoy the scenic views of the Waterfront. This four-and-a-half-acre neighborhood park has lush green lawns, fountains, and a small rose garden commemorating Rose Fitzgerald Kennedy. In the center of the park is a marble statue of explorer Christopher Columbus, with map in hand.

▶ **Long Wharf:** *The oldest continuously operating wharf in America was built in 1710 to accommodate maritime commerce. Long Wharf was one of the busiest ports in North America prior to the American Revolution.*

Rowes Wharf:
Formerly a pair of wharves, this modern complex is comprised of the luxurious Boston Harbor Hotel, condominiums, offices, and a marina, from where a water shuttle departs for Logan International Airport.

New England Aquarium: *The Aquarium's Giant Ocean Tank provides a multi-leveled view of sharks, sea turtles, and exotic fish, while the popular indoor Penguin Exhibit is home to penguins from all over the world. Visitors also enjoy the outdoor harbor seal exhibit and the sea-lion shows.*

The Living Room:
Just a short walk from Faneuil Hall and the North End, this unusual, quirky restaurant with love seats and couches has a great selection of seafood, a creative martini menu, and a Sunday morning Pajama Party Brunch. A 150-gallon tank overlooks the martini bar. Outdoor dining with a view over the waterfront is available in the summer.

◀ The Barking Crab:

A festive seafood restaurant popular among locals and tourists, the Barking Crab serves entrées on picnic tables, has ceiling light fans made of crab traps, and a great view of Boston Harbor and the skyline. Live outdoor music in the summertime provides fun entertainment.

▲ Christopher Columbus Park:

Immediately to the north of Long Wharf is Christopher Columbus Park. With its lush green lawns and fountains, this neighborhood park is a great place for a relaxing stroll and to enjoy the many scenic views along the waterfront.

◁ **Boston Fire Museum:**

This old firehouse is one of Boston's most unusual museums, displaying antique fire-fighting memorabilia and equipment from the Greater Boston area. The museum also educates and informs the public about fire safety.

△ **Boston Waterfront:**

Boston Harbor became a busy port for trade and immigration. The Boston Tea Party, which helped to precipitate the American Revolution, took place on its shores. Today Boston's waterfront is comprised of expensive condominiums, offices, and a marina.

North End

Over and around the chaos of the Big Dig and behind Faneuil Hall and Quincy Market is the North End, Boston's oldest neighborhood. This vibrant Italian enclave has retained its old-world character with its tightly clustered brick rowhouses, wrought-iron fire escapes, traditional Italian cafés and pastry shops, bakeries, greengrocers, and authentic restaurants. The North End takes on a festive atmosphere nearly every weekend during the summer with festivals to celebrate various saints, complete with marching bands and street vendors selling calamari and sausages.

The North End played an important role in Revolutionary history and holds three Freedom Trail sites: Old North Church, Paul Revere's house, and Copp's Hill Burying Ground. Old North Church was built in 1723 and is the oldest church in Boston. At Paul Revere's request, two lanterns were hung in Old North Church's steeple by a church sexton to warn the Minutemen that British forces were going to cross the Charles River by ship then march to Lexington and Concord. That night, April 18, 1775, Paul Revere left his small wooden house and set out on a legendary journey to beat the British to Lexington. Paul Revere's colonial house, located in North Square was built in 1680 and is the oldest remaining building in Boston.

Copp's Hill Burying Ground is the city's second-oldest cemetery and was developed on the highest hill of the Shawmut Peninsula in 1659. During the Battle of Bunker Hill, British soldiers used the cemetery's elevation to launch cannonballs at rebel forces, and used the gravestones for target practice. Panoramic views of Charlestown can be seen from the top of the hill on a clear day.

Hanover and Salem Streets make the North End a popular dining destination. Food from different regions of Italy can be found in more than 100 restaurants, from small eateries to more elegant restaurants. Both areas retain their neighborhood feel with small bakeries and greengrocers scattered about and locals chatting in Italian next to storefronts. Before the North End became "Little Italy", it was home to a number of European immigrants. The Irish came first, then the Germans, Russian and Polish Jews, and Portuguese fishermen. The influx of Italian immigrants began in the early 1900s, and by 1920, 90 percent of the population came from central and southern Italy. Today, approximately half of North End residents are of Italian descent.

▶ **Paul Revere's House:** *Built in 1680, Paul Revere's house is the oldest building in Boston and a National Historic Landmark. On April 18, 1775, rebel leader Paul Revere left from this wooden house to warn the Lexington and Concord residents of the imminent approach of British soldiers.*

▶ **Old North Church:**
The oldest church in Boston, Old North Church was built in 1723. On April 18, 1775, Paul Revere asked a church sexton to hang two lanterns in its steeple to warn colonists of the approach of the British soldiers prior to the start of the American Revolution. At 191 feet, the church's steeple is a major landmark.

▼ **Paul Revere Statue:**
Paul Revere is immortalized in this bronze sculpture, which is located on the Paul Revere Mall, also known as the Prado. Engraved plaques on the brick walls lining the Mall list the North End's famous residents and their accomplishments. Visitors walking the Freedom Trail enjoy relaxing in the tree-shaded promenade.

▶ **Old North Church Interior:** *Brass chandeliers rise high above box pews inside the white-painted interior of Old North Church. The box pews are still laid out as they were in colonial times, although they are not as tall. The names of family owners of the pews can be found engraved on bronze plates.*

Copp's Hill Burying Ground: *The second-oldest cemetery in Boston is the final resting place for nearly 11,000 colonial Bostonians. During the Battle of Bunker Hill, British soldiers fired cannonballs from atop the hill and used the gravestones for target practice. The cemetery is the highest point in the North End and views of the U.S.S. Constitution can be seen in the distance.*

Mamma Maria: *Set in a nineteenth-century brick rowhouse, this upscale restaurant serves Italian cuisine in intimate dining rooms that have views of historic North Square or the Boston skyline.*

Caffe Graffiti: *Locals and tourist socialize over espresso, cappuccino, and Italian pastries in this popular Hanover Street café. Some patrons chose to leave an imprint by signing a "brick" on the graffiti wall.*

◄ **Pizzeria Regina:**
Pizzeria Regina opened in 1926 behind a winding alley. Pizzas are still baked here in a brick oven using fresh, all-natural ingredients, and the meatballs and sausages are made from the owner's old family recipe.

▶ **All Saints' Way:**
Founded by a North End resident with a lifelong fascination with Catholic saints, All Saints' Way is located in a small private alley off Battery Street in the North End. There are intricate collages and thousands of portraits of saints inside the narrow walls of the brick passageway.

◄ **Feast of the Madonna:** *In an annual religious festival, a statue of the Madonna is paraded through the streets of the North End. The traditional procession is accompanied by a marching band and strolling revelers, who pin money to the Madonna's gown.*

Summer in the North End: *Hanover Street is Boston's haven for Italian restaurants, bakeries, and grocery shops. The best espresso, capuccino and Italian desserts in the city are found in the North End's cafés and pastry shops. Lively street festivals draw large crowds in July and August, while the distincly European atmosphere attracts locals and tourists year round.*

Hanover Street: *The most Italian street in Boston is lined with cafés, pastry shops, Italian restaurants, and residents going about their daily activities. It is most vibrant in the summer, when festivals take place to celebrate various saints.*

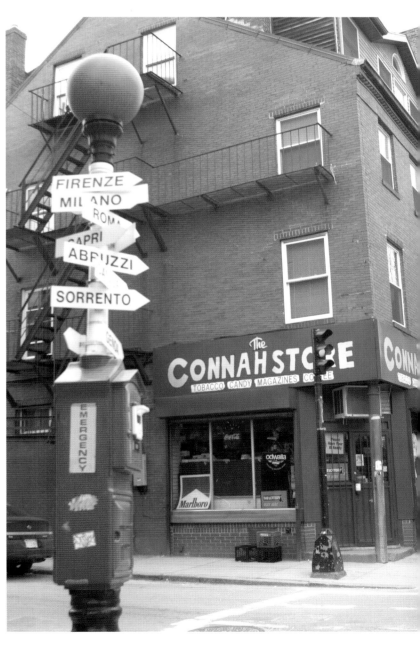

Charlestown

Across the Charles River from Boston is Charlestown, home to several historic sites from the American Revolution, best visited on the Freedom Trail. First settled by John Winthrop and about 1,000 Puritans in 1628, Charlestown became a bustling community that prospered from its waterfront location. Over the years, Charlestown grew into a working-class neighborhood. A 20-year urban renewal that began in the 1980s altered the landscape, yet still preserved the narrow, winding streets. Today, Charlestown has elegant properties with an Old World feel, as well as clapboard, triple-decker homes, and a few corner pubs.

The towering 221-feet-high Bunker Hill Monument looms high above Monument Square. It commemorates the most famous first battle of the American Revolution, fought on June 17, 1775. The battle actually took place on Breed's Hill, but the site was misnamed Bunker Hill. American troops, outnumbered by the British, were warned, "Don't fire until you see the whites of their eyes." The British won the bloody battle, but lost more than 1,000 soldiers, compared to 440 rebel forces. The Battle of Bunker Hill sent a clear message to the British that American colonists would fight until independence was won. The Bunker Hill Pavilion shows a spectacular multimedia presentation, entitled *Whites of Their Eyes*, which explains the Battle of Bunker Hill, complete with echoes of battle sounds. Bunker Hill Day is celebrated each year on June 17 at the monument and features street processions, battle re-enactments, and nineteenth-century-style carriages.

A climb up the 294 steps to the top of the Bunker Hill Monument affords panoramic views of Boston Harbor as well as a profile of the oldest warship afloat in the world, *U.S.S. Constitution*. Nicknamed "Old Ironsides" because cannonballs seemed to bounce off her in battle, the *U.S.S. Constitution* is permanently berthed at the Charlestown Navy Yard. Remarkably, the *U.S.S. Constitution* was never boarded by an enemy, captured 20 vessels, and remained undefeated in 42 battles.

▶ **U.S.S. Constitution:** *Built in the North End in 1797, the U.S.S. Constitution, nicknamed "Old Ironsides", is the oldest commissioned warship in the world. The U.S.S. Constitution is now berthed at Charlestown Navy Yard, where visitors can explore the ship and ask questions of guides dressed in period uniforms.*

◀ **Bunker Hill Monument:** *The 221-foot granite obelisk commemorates the Battle of Bunker Hill, one of the bloodiest battles of the Revolutionary War, fought on June 17, 1775. Charlestown Harbor and the U.S.S. Constitution's profile can be viewed from the top of the monument.*

▲ **Shuttle to Charlestown Navy Yard:** *A water shuttle service to Charlestown Navy Yard leaves from Long Wharf. One of the U.S. Navy's first shipyards, Charlestown Navy Yard, established in 1800, was the premier navy dockyard in America. Closed since 1974, it is now part of Boston National Historical Park.*

City Square: *When John Winthrop and the Puritans first arrived here from England, City Square is where they settled. A small public park marks the site of Winthrop's Town House, which was Boston's first seat of government.*

▶ ▶   **Leonard P. Zakim Bunker Hill Bridge:** *Part of the Big Dig project, this ten-lane bridge was named after a civil rights activist and American soldiers who fought British soldiers in the Battle of Bunker Hill. It is the widest suspension-cable bridge in the world.*

Cambridge

Cambridge is a city with an exciting, multi-cultural atmosphere packed with cafés, bookstores, museums, chic shops, street musicians, and students. Two of the world's most prestigious academic institutions—Harvard University and the Massachusetts Institute of Technology (MIT)—are just a few miles apart here. With a diverse population of nearly 100,000, Cambridge is an international community that has merged education, arts, and culture.

Originally called Newtowne, Cambridge was a quiet farming village founded by the Puritans in 1630. Newtowne was later renamed Cambridge after the English university town where many of Boston's early settlers were educated. Cambridge became a city in 1846 and established itself as the center for education and innovation. It is now known for its high-tech companies and biotechnology firms, many of which have been launched by MIT graduates.

Cambridge's cultural vibe can be found in and around Harvard Square. There are students and tourists on every corner of the square, street performers providing music and entertainment, and more bookstores than in any other city in the United States. Observe the colorful street scenes from one of more than 100 restaurants and sidewalk cafés. Nearby is the Charles River, an area filled with joggers, rollerbladers, and bikers year round, and with sun-worshippers in the summer. A short stroll from Harvard Square is the Longfellow National Historic Site, which is preserved just as it was when poet Henry Wadsworth Longfellow lived there.

The country's first college, Harvard, was founded in 1636, and named after its benefactor John Harvard. The college, which began in a wooden house behind a cow pasture, now has more than 400 buildings scattered throughout Cambridge and Boston. Harvard Yard is the tree-lined courtyard most seen in movies, and tourists come here to touch the statue of John Harvard for good luck. Close by is Cambridge Common, a public park where a plaque marks the elm tree under which George Washington gathered his troops in 1775.

The three Harvard University Art Museums—the Sackler, the Fogg, and the Busch-Reisinger—feature art collections of all styles and genres, and can be explored in an afternoon. A longer visit is required for the many galleries at the Harvard Museum of Natural History and the Peabody Museum of Archaeology and Ethnology.

Alongside the Charles River is the Massachusetts Institute of Technology (MIT), the world's leading university dedicated to the study of technology and scientific research. Millions of government dollars help fund MIT's research programs, which have produced instruments and guidance devices for NASA and the Department of Defense. In 2000, MIT commissioned world-renowned architect Frank Gehry to design the Stata Center, the most quirky academic building on campus, which looks as though it's straight out of a children's book. This whimsical three-dimensional structure is a sight not to be missed on a visit to Cambridge.

▶ **Harvard Square:** *Cambridge's vibrant epicenter is a haven for students, tourists, street musicians, and activists. Packed with sidewalk cafés, restaurants, and an abundance of bookstores, Harvard Square is lively almost every day of the week. The Harvard Coop dominates the Square, selling street-chic clothing, posters, and books. The other local landmark is Out of Town News, which stocks newspapers and magazines in several different languages.*

◄ **Harvard University:**

The oldest college in America was the only one in the New World until 1693. Some of Harvard Yard's oldest buildings date back to the eighteenth century, merging architecture from America's colonial past to the present. Harvard University is one of the finest academic institutions in the world for the study of arts, sciences, medicine, and law.

▲ **Holden Chapel at Harvard University:**

Completed in 1744, Holden Chapel started out as a chapel, but has been used for many different purposes over the years. It served as the barracks for colonial troops during the American Revolution and was the first home of Harvard Medical School. Today, its high-vaulted ceiling provides excellent acoustics for the building's use as a classroom and rehearsal space for Harvard choral groups.

◀ **Memorial Church at Harvard University:** *Until 1886, attendance at morning prayers was mandatory at Harvard University. Memorial Church, built in 1932, is Harvard's official place of worship and its 172-foot-high steeple topped with a pennant-shaped weathervane is a classic image of Harvard Yard. The church performs baptisms, weddings, and funerals and welcomes visitors.*

▶ **Cambridge Common:** *Cambridge Common has been the site of community events since early settlers used it as a cow pasture. Commemorative statues and objects from colonial history dot the southern corner of the park and include a statue of George Washington standing in the shade of the elm tree where he took control of the troops in 1775 and these cannons captured from the British when they evacuated Boston in 1776.*

▶ **Carpenter Center for Visual Arts:** *The Carpenter Center at Harvard University is the only building in America designed by French architect Le Corbusier. Its bold sculptural form and walkway leading to the building has drawn criticism from Harvard traditionalists. Yet, it's functional for classrooms, offices, and the art department, and two of New England's best contemporary art galleries also occupy the building.*

◀ **Fogg Art Museum:**
*Opened in 1895, the Fogg is
the oldest and most popular
of Harvard's three art
museums. Art collections
include the Impressionist
works of Monet and Renoir,
some Van Gogh self-portraits,
and a collection of Picasso's
work. Inside the Fogg is the
Busch-Reisinger Museum,
which showcases artwork of
the German Expressionists
and modern art from Central
and Northern Europe.*

▶ **Sackler Museum:**
*Exhibiting works from Asian,
Indian, and Islamic cultures,
the Sackler Museum's
treasures include Roman
sculpture, Greek vases,
Japanese woodblock prints,
Chinese jades, Korean
ceramics, Muslim texts,
ancient coins, lacquer boxes,
narrative paintings, and an
array of Buddhist sculptures.
Some of the exhibits rotate
every other month.*

▶▶ **Charles River at
Cambridge:** *Visitors and
locals alike are drawn to the
Charles River Esplanade,
a popular area for biking,
jogging, roller-blading, sailing,
and relaxing. Every October,
the Charles River is the site
of the world's largest two-
day rowing event, Head of
the Charles Regatta, when
nearly 7,000 athletes from
around the world compete in
two days of race events that
attract around 300,000
spectators.*

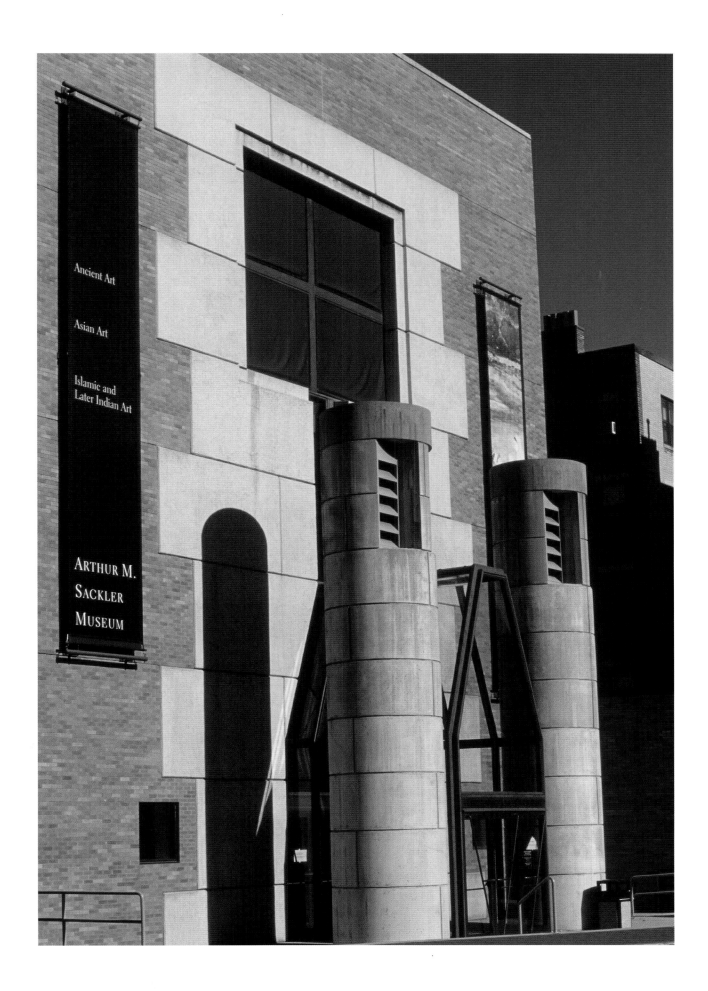

◀ **Longfellow National Historic Site:** *This mansion was used as George Washington's headquarters during the siege of Boston in 1775. Years later, it became the home of poet Henry Wadsworth Longfellow, who received it as a wedding gift.*

Longfellow lived here for 40 years until his death in 1882. The original nineteenth-century furnishings are preserved in the house, and its walls are still adorned with Longfellow's art collection and works from famous writers in his literary circle.

▲ **Peabody Museum of Archaeology and Ethnology:** *Founded in 1866, this museum is dedicated to the study of indigenous people and civilizations from around the world. Artifacts discovered on Harvard-led anthropology*

and archaeology expeditions are displayed, as well as wax dummies in traditional garb. One of the most impressive artifacts is a huge cast of a Mayan temple stairwell, which has the longest hieroglyphics text in the world.

MCMXVI

SACHVSETTS   INSTITVTE   OF   TECHNOL

▲ **Massachusetts Institute of Technology:** *Founded in 1861, the Massachusetts Institute of Technology—MIT—has become one of the world's leading universities in engineering and science. It* *occupies more than 150 acres and has 10,000 students enrolled. MIT graduates are on the cutting edge of the information-technology revolution and often launch their own successful companies.*

▶ **Stata Center at MIT:** *The Ray and Maria Stata Center at MIT is regarded as one of world-renowned architect Frank Gehry's most creative works to date. The premise behind the unusual design was to create a* *freethinking environment for students and faculty in an effort to promote new ideas and innovative research. Inside the Stata Center are flexible research facilities, classrooms, a large auditorium, a health club, and a childcare center.*

In and Around Boston

By the mid-nineteenth century, Boston's only green spaces were Boston Common and the Public Garden. Frederick Law Olmstead, acknowledged as the founder of American landscape architecture, changed the look of this old colonial city in 1850. He designed the Emerald Necklace, a continuous seven-mile string of nine parks originating from Boston Common to the Public Garden, Commonwealth Avenue Mall, Back Bay, and the Arnold Arboretum, before ending at Franklin Park.

The Fens was marshland before it became a jewel in the Emerald Necklace. It now houses two of the city's most important art museums, the Museum of Fine Arts and the Isabella Stewart Gardner Museum. The Fens also separates Kenmore Square and the Fenway neighborhoods. Kenmore Square is identified by its landmark Citgo sign, Boston University students, and cheap eateries and bars. Around the corner is Fenway Park, home to the much-loved Boston Red Sox. A visit to the historic park feels like a step back in time. Tours take you to the playing field, the Green Monster (the left field wall), and the manually operated scoreboard.

The John F. Kennedy Library and Museum overlooks Boston Harbor from the Columbia Point peninsula in Dorchester. Noted architect I.M. Pei designed the stunning white concrete-and-glass building, which houses a permanent exhibition of films of JFK press conferences, the president's desk, and other Kennedy family memorabilia.

Zoo New England encompasses Franklin Park Zoo and Stone Zoo. Originally planned for a small menagerie, Franklin Park Zoo now houses more than 220 species of animals. Exhibits such as the Butterfly Landing, with more than 1,000 fluttering butterflies, and the Tropical Forest, which features a gorilla exhibit, pygmy hippos, and tropical birds, are among the zoo's main attractions. The smaller Stone Zoo has a Touchable Barnyard, llamas, monkeys, porcupine, and flamingos, along with other animals of the wild.

The Arnold Arboretum is a living botany museum with more than 15,000 exotic trees, shrubs, and plants. Run by Harvard University, it is located in Jamaica Plain. Miniature bonsai trees have been at the Arboretum since 1937, and flowers are guaranteed to bloom from late March into November. Lilac Sunday, the third Sunday in May, is a popular annual event celebrating the arrival of 400 lilacs in full bloom—one of the largest collections in the world.

The Boston Beer Museum, also in Jamaica Plain, offers tours that lead you through the original Sam Adams Brewery. The beer was named after Revolutionary war hero, Sam Adams, in hopes of starting a "revolution" to sway Americans from imported beers. Visitors receive a sample of the beer in a plastic commemorative pint glass.

▶ **John F. Kennedy National Historic Site:** *The childhood home of the 35th President of the United States is located in Brookline, MA, and is now a National Historic Site. The house represents the humble beginnings of one of America's most prominent political families.*

▲ **Isabella Stewart Gardner Museum:** *Boston socialite Isabella Stewart Gardner welcomed visitors to her stunning Venetian palazzo-style mansion in 1903 to view her personal collection of fine art and furnishings. The museum houses more than 2,500 paintings, sculptures, tapestries, and rare books, and has remained unchanged since its founder's death in 1924.*

▷ **Museum of Fine Arts:** *Opened in 1876, the Museum of Fine Arts is the largest museum in New England. Internationally known for its collection of French Impressionist paintings, Egyptian artifacts, Greek vases, Paul Revere silver bowls, Japanese art, and musical instruments, the museum houses more than one million objects in its elegant galleries.*

▽ **Fenway Park:** *The nation's oldest and smallest baseball stadium opened in 1912. Fenway Park is home to the Boston Red Sox. Every part of the baseball park has a story and tours recount its legendary history.*

John F. Kennedy Library and Museum: *The striking concrete-and-glass structure designed by renowned architect I.M. Pei pays tribute to former U.S. President John F. Kennedy's life and legacy. The library opened in 1993 and houses extensive artifacts, exhibits, and television footage of the Kennedy presidency.*

Arnold Arboretum: *Home to one of the largest collections of flora and fauna in the world, with more than 15,000 labeled specimens, the Arnold Arboretum is the oldest arboretum is the US. It also serves as a public park.*

Index

Boston Map

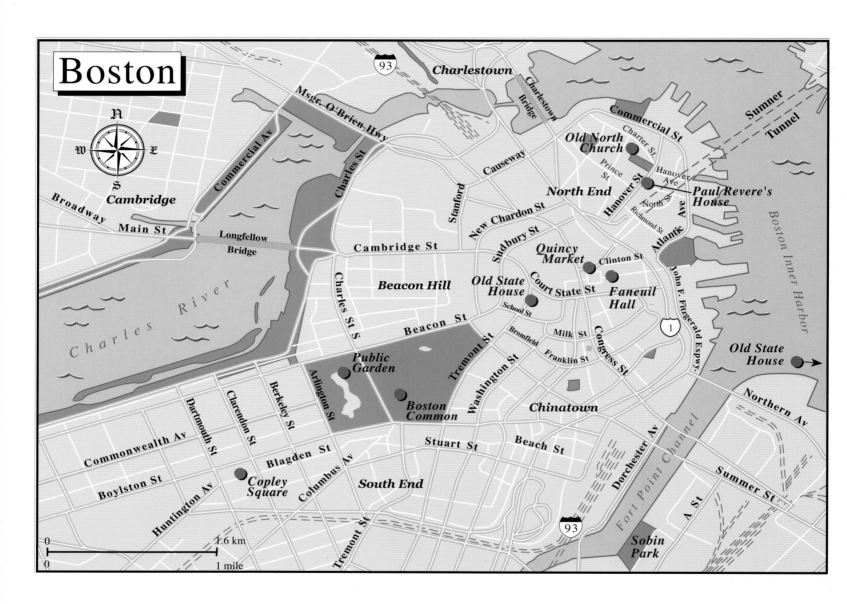

Boston

Charlestown

Msgr. O'Brien Hwy

Commercial Av

Charles St

Cambridge

Broadway

Main St

Longfellow Bridge

Charles River

Cambridge St

Charles St S

Beacon Hill

Beacon St

Public Garden

Arlington St

Boston Common

Tremont St

Washington St

Berkeley St

Clarendon St

Dartmouth St

Commonwealth Av

Blagden St

Columbus Av

Copley Square

Boylston St

Huntington Av

South End

Tremont St

Stuart St

Beach St

Charlestown Bridge

Causeway

Stanford

New Chardon St

Sudbury St

Old North Church

Charter St

Prince St

North St

North End

Hanover St

Hanover Ave

Richmond St

Paul Revere's House

Atlantic Av

Quincy Market

Clinton St

Old State House

Court St

State St

School St

Faneuil Hall

Milk St

Bromfield

Franklin St

Congress St

Chinatown

John F. Fitzgerald Expwy.

Old State House

Northern Av

Dorchester Av

Fort Point Channel

A St

Summer St

Sobin Park

Sumner Tunnel

Boston Inner Harbor

0 — 1.6 km

0 — 1 mile